Silversmithing

A Beginners Guide to Designs, Techniques, and Methods for Jewelry Makers

1st Edition

By Olive Montgums

Copyright

Table of Contents

Introduction

I want to thank you and congratulate you for purchasing the book, *"Silversmithing: A Beginners Guide to Designs, Techniques and Methods for Jewelry Makers"*.

This book contains proven steps and strategies on how to become efficient in silversmithing.

Silver, a part from being beautiful, is a valuable metal, which has been used for trade and decoration for over a thousand years. Many nations has been using silver as their primary form of currency throughout history. Today, silver is popularly used for both decoration and jewelry.

Through the years, silver was usually used for household purposes such as cutlery, bowls, candlesticks, and other tableware. These items were often used as gifts or dowry of marriages in Europe and passed down from one generation to another. Most of these items are often displayed in art exhibitions and museums, which provide a testament of the skills of silversmiths. In the past, only the rich could dream of having a silver article or object given its high value. In the Americas, huge deposits of silver were discovered in the recent years and made the metal widely available as a necessity or luxury item.

Silversmiths who work with silver and other precious metals are highly trained. More often than not, they were apprentices of another silversmith during their younger years. The craft of silversmithing, on the other hand, requires skill, strength, and intelligence. This is why a number of silversmiths have founded professional guilds to protect the secrets of their trade.

Silver is either hammered into shape, extruded into wires, cast in molds, stamped, pressed, or cut. These silversmithing techniques are limitless and available to skilled silversmiths. Today, some specialized tools were developed for silversmithing. These include various types of files and hammers, anvils, torches, cutting tools, and a range of polishing compounds and chemicals among others. There are also techniques and tools for turning a piece of silver into a jewelry item. For instance, there are sets of tools available for making chains or setting gems/stones.

More often than not, silversmiths work with silver at room temperature as it is quite malleable; however, it is necessary for the silversmithing process to have certain types of heat treatment to keep the silver from becoming brittle. The room temperature is also a factor for using techniques such as casting. Coins and other articles that have detailed designs are usually pressed in a mold. This is to keep the details of the articles intact.

In general, modern silver articles are made of sterling silver, which consists of an alloy of 92.5% silver and 7.5% copper. The alloy of silver and copper makes the final product harder and long-lasting. Usually, silver jewelry is plated or "flashed" with pure silver or other valuable metals to provide the jewelry with the preferred finish. Some other alloys used today include Argentium sterling and Brittania silver, both have their respective properties, although they are less common as compared to sterling silver.

People still use silver for making fine jewelry and home goods. It is enormously popular in Western styles, specifically in the combination of turquoise and leather. Silver is also used in a number of prizes and awards such as rodeo bet buckles, commemorative coins, trophies, and medals.

A skilled silversmith can silver-plate less valuable metals such as copper or steel in order to come up with a more desirable item at a lower cost. However, silver-plating on less valuable metals provides the same appearance as that with fine silver, depending on the skills of the silversmith.

Although silver workers no longer have guilds, they are still guided by standardized alloy formulas and raw-material prices. They still follow regulations that protect consumers, who can expect that sterling silver items have the quality they deserve. The work of a silversmith is the result of years of experience and should be treasured as a piece of art.

Silversmithing is an art of crafting silver into a beautiful piece of jewelry or other things. It is an art, which fine-tunes and hones silver to create something precious, functional, or both.

Back in the days, silversmiths focused on creating flatware, holloware, jewelry and other things that are commonly found in homes. These include knives, forks, spoons, jewelry, cups, pitchers, bowls, urns, decorative plates, and sculpture among others. Silversmiths often concentrated on the functionality of their creations instead of necklaces and other accessories although some also crafted precious or luxurious pieces.

Silversmiths used bars or sheets of silver to create various shapes depending on their desired product. They used specific tools for different silversmithing techniques. In general, the bar or sheet of silver would be hammered out while it is at room temperature. The silver needed to be hardened, bent, and annealed periodically to prevent from cracking during the entire process of crafting. To anneal means to apply heat to soften the silver to become pliable.

For over a hundred years, silversmithing is a source of fruitful employment. For instance, in the North Eastern part of United Kingdom during the late 1600s, it was a requirement to finish a full seven-year apprenticeship in operating a shop to be able to call oneself as a silversmith. Silversmiths also looked for potential silver workers also for a period of seven years prior to sending them out to become professionals.

Also in the 1600s, a number of silversmiths from Europe were inspired to flock to the United States to create pieces that are more modern. This started America's industrialization in terms of silver.

Silversmithing, apart from being a craft, is a talent that should be given high regard as it has a remarkable place in the history of artisanship and arts. In this book, you will find out how valuable silversmithing is. This book discusses not only the techniques used in silversmithing, but also the basics of becoming proficient in silversmithing through learning the fundamentals of silver and its sources; how to appraise or assay silver ores; and cupellation of silver ores. This book also discusses the alloys of silver and its various qualities; the uses and applications of silver solders; melting of silver; how to work on the silver; and enriching silver surfaces.

Thanks again for choosing this book, I hope you enjoy it!

Chapter 1: The Fundamentals of Silver

Characteristics

While gold is the finest metal according to most people, pure silver comes next although it is smoother and more polished in nature. Silver is also regarded as malleable; however, it does not extend or yield easily under the hammer as compared to fine gold. Silver, being a malleable metal is characterized by its color, which is perfectly white. In fact, it is the whitest among all metals. In its pure state, silver is thoroughly soft that you can even cut it using a dull knife. However, when crafted properly, silver is harder than gold.

Given that silver is extremely soft during its pure state, filigree work is employed to take out its elasticity specifically when it is alloyed. The Indian filigree workers, who are considered as the finest across the globe, are keen when it comes to silver's absolute purity prior to manufacturing their work as it is extremely soft in its pure state.

Fine silver is also exceedingly ductile; you can stretch it out into the finest wire without it breaking and becoming annealed. The purity of silver is usually discerned through annealing.

The color of fine silver does not change even when it is heated. Thus, when silver contains alloy, its color darkens when heated and comes in contact with air. It also hardens immediately in wire-drawing.

In ancient times, silver was known as a metallic element and is mentioned repeatedly in the Holy Bible. During the time of the patriarchs, silver was involved in various transactions as it was used as a standard of value. This is why it became a circulating medium of exchange, which continued to the present day.

Silver, as token money, was discerned as a circulating medium of trade. For instance, the Egyptian symbol for the metal is the moon, while in chemistry, the symbol is *Ag*, which comes from the Latin term, *argentunity*, meaning silver.

When fine silver is polished, it does not produce the luster that other highly polished metals do. Its luster is inferior although it reflects more heat and light as compared to other metals without changing its color for a long period. This is the reason why silver is usually used for various purposes apart from luxury and ornament. Its color remains the same for a considerable period and highly resistant to oxidation, which makes it ideal for domestic purposes. Unlike gold, silver does not resist sulpheretted hydrogen as such process can make it tarnish easily, especially when it is left exposed in damp areas.

Silver is also next to gold when it comes to ductility and malleability. In its pure sate, its specific gravity or density is between 10.47 and 10.50 depending on the level of compression in received from hammering and rolling. When placed under full red heat, silver is completely fusible as it has extremely low radiating power for heat. Consequently, silver wires can retain and conduct heat better than other metals. When silver is subjected to enormously high temperature in the lire, it volatilizes and emits greenish fumes.

When it comes to hardness, it is positioned between the levels of gold and copper. When a small part of gold is added to silver, its quality increases, which makes it useful in the arts. The perfect solvent for silver is nitric acid given that it dissolves it rapidly and easily, forming nitrate of silver that is usually used for medical functions and in art as well. Hydrochloric and sulfuric acids act upon silver much slower in the cold as compared to nitric acid.

Silver partially resists the best aqua-regia, which is caused by the dense chloride forming on its surface, specifically from the process of mixing hydrochloric acid with aqua-regia.

More often than not, fine silver is used in commercial and industrial arts, fine filigree work, and silver lace manufacturing. All nations make use of fine silver with a small addition of alloy for the purpose of coinage. This is because silver fuses easily with other metals although it is used in alloys for the purpose of silversmithing and watchmaking arts. The price of fine silver for the purpose of manufacturing depends on the troy weight and value of the total quantity purchased. The silver ores of commerce generally have an intermixture of a small part of gold. However, some silver ores manufacture without a proper chemical investigation, which results to loss brought about by the omission that could have paid the expenses of the process.

Silver dissolves when it goes through hot and concentrated sulfuric acid. This application is one of the most used methods for silver. When sulfuric acid is applied to gold, it would not have an effect. Silver resists the powerful effects of saltpeter or niter and resists caustic alkaline as compared to other metals apart from gold. Thus, its superiority for the production of utensils and other domestic purposes is high. In addition, given that is is metal, it resists vegetable acids.

Sources of Silver

In the United Kingdom, silver mining does not have a distinct operation given that the country does not have a huge quantity of silver ore. In the British Isles, the average annual yield for silver has been equal to 800, 000 ounces. This production is only next to Spain and the United States. The primary sources of silver in the British Isles from lead ores come from Isle of Man, Cornwall, Devonshire, Cardiganshire, and Montgomeryshire.

Silver is also produced in other non-prominent counties in the British Isles, including Cumberland, Northumberland, Flintshire, Durham, and Derbyshire. However, the percentage of silver ores in these counties is much smaller than the areas mentioned previously. Ireland also produces a reasonable amount of silver.

The primary source of silver in Europe is Spain where genuine silver ore is found. Saxony, Prussia, and England are also sources of silver where ores are associated chiefly with lead. Austria also has silver where ores are associated with copper. More often than not, silver is found near lead and copper mines although in small quantities.

The United States has a supply of silver of more than three-fourths of the total supply across the globe. This is because most of the territories in the United States are said to be argentiferous. The state of Nevada produces large supplies of silver as another mine was recently discovered although Mexico also yields the largest percentages of silver.

The value of silver is now depreciating considerably due to the extensive production of mines along with other causes. This is one of the reasons why silver is now primarily used in the arts and manufactures.

Analysis of Silver Ores (Assay)

A huge portion of the commerce of silver comes from ores through a process referred to as amalgamation. The ore is founded on the silver's read solubility in metallic mercury an mixed with common salt. After which, the ore is roasted. Through the employment of this method, the silver is reduced to a chloride state.

The roasting takes place in a reverberatory furnance wherein the heat is raised gradually and the ore, stirred constantly. The heat is increased just enough to raise the ore to an ample red heat. The ore is then placed into wooden barrels, which revolve in iron axles. Scraps of iron are added; thus, both the ore and iron scraps agitate together in a rotating motion. The effect of this motion is to reduce the silver's chloride content to a metallic state. Then, the ore is agitated with mercury, forming a fluid amalgam with the metal and other metallic ingredients that may be present during the roasting process. In order to recover the silver, the mercury is displaced by heat and the silver is left in an impure state.

Methods of Assaying Silver Ores

There are three ways of analyzing or assaying silver ores. These include melting in a crucible, scorification, and cupellation.

Crucible Assay

In this method, the ore is usually run down with an appropriate flux such as carbonate, charcoal, litharge, and borax. Practical assayers require these substances in the treatment of regular silver ores.

When it comes to assaying genuine silver ores, that is, if the ores contain little earthy matter, they may be treated through fusing with carbonate and borax in a crucible or melting pot. The size of the crucible should be about 4.5 inches tall and 2.5 inches wide. An amount of litharge, which is an oxide of lead and a semi-vitrious substance is added to induce fusion as well as collect all ingredients in a mass at the crucible's bottom. The ore should be well-pounded when put into the crucible and mixed with the following chemicals, which include 240 grains of pounded silver ore, 800 grains of litharge, 700 grains of carbonate, 300 grains of borax, and 50 grains of charcoal.

During the preparation of the mixture, two crucibles are warmed. Then, 100 grains of more litharge are powdered over the contents of the crucible. The second mixture is also prepared in the same way, placing both crucibles in the furnace and putting sufficient carbonate around them. The mixtures are either melted in a melting furnace or ordinary wind, which is usually used by jewelers in preparing their artwork. At first, the fusion takes place gradually as the combination of silver and lead is volatile when put in high temperature. Then, the fusion may be put in low heat for 25 minutes. The operation is completed with a full red heat for a little over 5 minutes.

During the fusion of the ingredients, one of the bricks on top of the furnace may be removed to see if the whole mass has liquified. The furnace may also be tapped once or twice in a light manner to procure the liquidation of the ingredients. Then, the mixture is poured immediately into an iron mold, which is warmed and greased previously to prevent spitting and adhesion.

The mold is set aside for a short period to cool. Once it is cool enough, it is plunged into a vessel of cold water. During the cooling period, metallic elements are found in the bottom and the slag is removed using a hammer, tapping it on the edge. Plunging the mold in cold water allows the separation of the elements. The mold is then cupelled to separate the silver from the lead as well as other elements that may be present.

Scorification

Silver ores that contain chemical combinations of metallic substances and sulfur of other metals may be assayed through the process of scorification. Scorification is also applicable to all types of argentiferous ores and considered as the most exact way of extracting silver from its ores. In the same manner as fusion with litharge, scorification also produces an alloy and requires cupellation.

In the scorification process, the ore should be pounded well and placed in a small vessel, which is shallow and made of close-grained refractory fire-clay. An ample amount of borax and finely granulated lead is added in the ore. The size of the scorifier or fusing cup should be about 1.5 inches tall and 2.5 inches wide, although some assayers use deeper scorifiers, similar to the shape of an egg. The purpose of such shape is to preserve the molten metal at the bottom. The scorifier should be well-covered as well as protected by the slag during the entire scorification process.

The principles applied in scorification are the exact opposite of the crucible assay. For instance, the goal of crucible assay is to reduce lead to a metallic state while in scorification, the metallic lead is added to the well-pounded ore and oxidized through fusion with air. In scorification, the ingredients include 60 grains of well-pounded ore, 600 finely granulated lead, 100 grains of borax, and 5 grains of powdered anthracite.

The scorifiers are charged in a systematic manner. First, the silver ore is mixed well with 300 grains of granulated lead. Then, the mixture is placed in the scorifier, adding the remaining amount of granulated lead. Burnt borax is placed on top of the mixture. Second, the scorifier is placed in an ordinary muffle or assay furnace. The strongest heat is applied to the scorifier for about 30 minutes. The first 15 minutes of the process is crucial, which is why the muffle-door should be kept closed so air would not enter.

Upon opening the muffle-door, it is expected for a current of air to pass through the furnace. This would convert an amount of the lead into litharge and combined with the earthy portions of the silver ore, other metallic sulphides, and the borax. Consequently, this produces a fusible slag on the metallic bath's surface, which extends over the entire surface of the scorifier. This flux protects the excess of lead from oxidization of the currents of air that went into the furnace. The remains are collected with the silver present in the ore and converted into a metallic state.

The process of scorification is continued for a little over 30 minutes or until the flux or slag is reduced into its liquid state. To facilitate the operation, the mixture should be stirred well with an iron rod to prevent it from becoming a hardened mass. When the flux or slag is liquid, you need to wrap it in a piece of paper with powdered anthracite. Then, it is dropped into the scorifier while it is still in the muffle or furnace. The purpose of adding anthracite is to reduce any portion of the metal that remains in the slag and separate them from the bulk.

More often than not, it would take 5 minutes for the anthracite to burn off. At this point, the operation is complete and the scorifier may be withdrawn from the fire immediately. The contents should also be poured in a casting mold. This would result to a button of silver lead.

When the mold cools, the metallic mass is taken out from the flux or slag using a hammer. The slag is then subjected to the cupellation process. If there is no sufficient borax present, the assayer would look for an infusible skin that floats on the surface. When a chloride of silver ore is set to be assayed, carbonate should be added to prevent sublimation. More borax should be added if there is infusible skin on the surface to dissolve impurity.

Cupellation

The process of cupellation is commonly done in a reverberatory furnace of a specific construction. The cupel used on the large scale differs from an ordinary one as it is larger in size. The cupel consists of a sturdy oval wrought iron ring. The full shape is discarded to prevent lead from overflowing during the process. The iron ring, also referred to as the test ring, contains the cupel. The frame of the test ring is about 60 inches long, 40 inches wide, and 6 inches deep. It is strengthened through a considerable number of broad iron strips, which are lined across the bottom. The cupel is prepared through working up finely ground bone ash and a little amount of carbonate of potash, both dissolved in water. Consequently, water is applied in a small amount at a time to the bone ash. Potash of about 2% is applied to mix with the bone ash and water.

The iron frame is filled with the bone ash, potash, and water mixture, and then pressed down into a solid mass with a hollowed center using a small trowel. The sides of the iron frame should be sloping towards the concave shape in the center. The hollow center should not extend more than 1 to 1.5 inches of the frame's bottom and the iron bars' top.

The hearth of the furnace is formed through the cupel. It should also be removable as it is not a part of the furnace. The hearth is set aside for several days to cool and dry. Once it is ready, it would require wedging in the place below the furnace's arch.

During the cupellation process, the fire should be moderate and the furnace should be raised slowly in temperature. If the cupel is heated to quickly, the cupel would tend to break or crack.

The hearth or bone ash cupel is then placed in an iron car after increasing temperature. Wind from a nozzle fan is required to facilitate the removal of the hearth. Once the hearth is set in place in the iron car, the latter should run below the furnace' vault on rails. Allowing wind or current of air to enter the furnace facilitates oxidation of the excess lead combined with the silver. This produces litharge on the molten mass' surface. When the litharge is formed, it is blown forward through the blast and passes a gap in the mouth of the cupel into a movable iron pot.

The proportions of the metals in the cupel is altered through continuous oxidation of the lead.

Thus, the cupel should be kept full of lead ore, which takes it in its fused state. In addition, about 500 to 600 pounds of metal should be kept constantly in the hearth or bone ash cupel. When the silver increases, it should be withdrawn occasionally to make way for further production of lead ore.

The process of cupellation is employed when the silver increases from 2,000 to 3,000 ounces to the ton and may be executed through drilling a hole beneath the cupel, allowing the silver to flow into a receptacle that would receive it. The operations done in the furnace are stopped while employing this procedure. The hole beneath the cupel should be closed up once the withdrawal of silver is done. A moistened bone ash may be used to close the hole.

The process may be repeated by adding 500 to 600 pounds of lead ore to the lead ore. More often than not, a single cupel lasts up to 48 hours and about six to seven tons of lead may be set for oxidization.

When the process of cupellation is prolonged, it can increase the richness of the alloy that may remain and such silver-lead alloy would be set again for a second cupellation process.

Silver Alloys

Fine silver is compatible with almost all useful metals; however, its most significant alloys are those from copper given that the former is more appropriate for the production of the work of a silversmith than other substances. Copper also generates a more pleasant effect with regard to finish. Silver objects tend to have an elegant appearance, especially those of the filigree kinds and those with good designs.

Before discussing the alloys of silver, it is important to note what an alloy is. Alloy is the combination of two or more metals through fusion, forming a metallic compound. The number of metallic elements in a specific alloy is unlimited and may be in any proportion, although it should be remembered that these elements would be combined chemically. On the other hand, mercury is an exception given that the mixing it with another element results in an amalgam.

There are about forty-nine metals according to the field of chemistry; however, the number of metals, which are applicable for industrial art is less than twenty. These include gold, copper, platinum, nickel, mercury, tin, antimony, silver, zinc, aluminum, iron, lead, arsenic, and bismuth. Some of these metals are applied occasionally for special arts purposes, specifically when they are in their pure state.

If hardness is a requirement or a distinguished characteristic for a certain industrial or arts purpose, a combination of two or more metals may be employed in various proportions. This may be done through stirring and fusion, resulting in a particular alloy.

Only few applications in both industrial and arts pursuits require metals in their pure state. This is because most metals, including gold and silver are too soft. Other metals, including bismuth, antimony, and arsenic are too brittle to be used for manufacturing purposes. It is possible to make use of thousands of alloys; however, there are only about 300 alloys that are proven to be successful for commercial use.

As mentioned earlier in this section, the principal alloy of silver is copper; although nickel and zinc are also employed occasionally for ordinary qualities of silver. Tin is often used in preparing solder for commoner silver qualities for easier fusion.

More often than not, combining silver with copper is done in various proportions through melting and stirring them together while in their fused state. The outcome will, naturally, become different in physical character from fine silver, specifically in terms of malleability and ductility. On the other hand, the compound produced from the combination of silver and copper is harder and more elastic. Thus, it is more adaptable for use in manufacturing or industrial purposes. In addition, it is more durable for use in the works of a silversmith.

Copper

Just like other precious metals, copper is known to have existed during the ancient times. In fact, even in the Holy Bible, particularly in the Old Testament, copper was mentioned as was of the six metals. Historians also discerned it as one of the seven metals used by an ancient philosopher.

Alchemists gave the name Venus to this metal. Venus is one of the principal planets with an orbit located between Mercury and the Earth. Copper's scientific name is *cuprum*, which is derived from the Isle of Cyprus. This is the place where the Greeks discovered the system of mining.

Copper is found in almost all parts of the world; although a considerable amount of copper is found in the United Kingdom.

Copper has a reddish color and is tenacious, ductile, and malleable. More often than not, it is used for alloying gold and silver for manufacturing of jewelry and other objects. In terms of malleability, copper is next to both gold and silver in the useful metals list. When it comes to ductility, it is in the fifth rank and next to iron in terms of tenacity.

On the other hand, copper does not work so well with fire given that if subjected to heat for a long period, it loses a substantial part of its substance. As such, silver alloys, including copper should be looked out for in the crucible to prevent losing their respective substances when subjected to heat.

When copper is struck, it generates a feeble sound, and easily abrades when subjected to a hand tool such as the file. Under white heat, it fuses at about 1994 degrees Fahrenheit. When rolled and hammered, it yields a gravity of 8.96 and 8.88 for cast copper. When in water, its weight is reduced between 1/8th and 1/9th.

When copper is exposed to a damp weather, it produces a greenish oxide referred to as verdigris. This is why silver articles that contain copper result in discoloration when left exposed to various weather conditions. When copper is heated and comes in contact with air, it oxidizes and scales fall off from it when touched.

Zinc

This metal is also referred to as spelter when it is in its pure state. Today, however, it is no longer used often for alloying silver; however, it is commonly used in preparing silver for the process of soldering. Professional silversmiths know the appropriate proportions, qualities, and combinations when using zinc as an alloy of silver or for soldering. More often than not, zinc is used for industrial purposes.

When in its pure state, zinc has a bluish white color. It is hard and extremely transparent. On the other hand, when it is subjected to a heat of about 250 to 300 degrees Fahrenheit, it becomes malleable and safe for hammering and rolling.

In terms of malleability, zinc ranks eighth among metals. It ranks seventh both in terms of tenacity and ductility. It has a symbol of *Zn* in chemistry. Commercially, its value in its pure state is about 4d. per pound.

Nickel

Nickel is a kind of metal that is found mainly in the Hartz Mountains. Germans used to call it "Kupfer nickel" or false copper. The term, nickel means detraction. Cronstedt paved way for the discovery of nickel more than a century ago.

This metal is greyish-white in color and said to be magnetic in the same manner as steel and iron. When subjected to heat of about 600 degrees Fahrenheit, it loses a part of its property. Its specific gravity ranges between 8.40 and 8.50, depending on the degree of compression it receives. Nickel is brittle, although it may be rolled flat, drawn into sheets or wires.

When it comes to silversmithing and jewelry-making, nickel is less ductile and harder as compared to other metals. In terms of hardness, it is next to iron and produces distinct brightness when polished. In terms of malleability, it stands next to iron and tenth in the database of useful metals. When it comes to ductility, it ranks tenth as well.

Nickel is said to be extremely infusible. It does not tarnish or oxidize easily when placed under ordinary temperatures. Some countries use this metal in manufacturing small coins for currency; however, today, its use for such purpose seemed to be abandoned.

Nickel alloys are now being used in some other manufacturing purposes given that it forms a hard white alloy that is ideal for generating electroplate. More often than not, silver is deposited in electroplates. Nickel is also used in other silver allows for maintaining the whiteness of the silver. Furthermore, nickel is also used in imitating or replacing silver in the manufacturing of commercial wares although it is combined with other metals. It becomes a more useful alloy when combined with zinc, tin, and copper as it results in great hardness.

Tin

This metal is said to be the oldest known metal, which was used in combination with copper in the ancient Egyptian arts. Tin is white in color and its luster is almost the same as that of silver. However, tin tarnishes more quickly that other alloys of silver.

Tin is considered as the lightest of all metals except for zinc and aluminum. It has a density of about 7.0 to 7.3 regardless with it is hammered, rolled, or cast. The abundance of tin is said to be found in Cornwall where it was obtained during the time of the Phoenicians.

Tin has an unstable nature just like silver and gold, although it melts in moderate heat even before it is subjected to red hot fire of about 442 degrees Fahrenheit. When this metal is kept for a long time in fire with exposure to the air, it oxidizes rapidly. Moreover, it dissolves when acted upon with nitric, sulfuric, and hydrochloric acids. When tin is in water, it loses weight of more than $1/7^{th}$ from its absolute weight when in air.

On the other hand, tin is not advisable to be alloyed with gold and silver given that it results in extreme brittleness. This is especially true with silver, which when alloyed with tin, becomes totally disqualified for a silversmith's work. However, tin is still considered as an alloy of silver given that it is useful for soldering and filing into dust. It induces faster fusion; yet, if it can be helped, tin should still not be used for any silversmith's works. This is because it generates vapors that result in permanent injuries in a person working with it. Thus, if possible, melting alloys of silver should be avoided specifically in the introduction of scrap tin in the furnace.

Tin is extremely malleable, tenacious, and moderately ductile. It ranks fifth on the list in terms of malleability and eighth in terms of tenacity and ductility. Its modern scientific name of tin is *Sn*. Its Egyptian symbol or mark was the same as the sign of Jupiter, which relates it to the planet's brightness. Even in mythology, tin represents the supreme deity of the Romans and the Greeks.

Chapter 2: Qualities of Silver

In the previous chapter, the physical and chemical properties of fine silver for special purposes were discussed, particularly when it is in pure state. In this chapter, however, the qualities of silver will be discussed in terms of its commercial uses as a metal.

The manufacture of fine filigree work is considered as one of the industries that have great demand for pure silver. Fine filigree is a type of silversmith's work, which was revived in Europe, specifically in London and Birmingham during the years 1864 to 1865. However, the success of fine filigree work did not last long due to Eastern competitors, whom produced more excellent specimens of fine wire-working and filigree art. For instance, in India, filigree work is carried out exceptionally, resulting to the magnificent silver products of natives who practiced the craft. Most of the silver products created in the Eastern parts of the world depicted nature in various forms, including animals, flowers, and ophidians among others. Given that the workman's ability is thoroughly skillful, the representation of the fine filigree work is likewise splendid.

As mentioned in the previous chapter, when a filigree craftsman works on silver, the metal should be in its absolute pure state. This is because when it is on its finest, silver is tremendously pliable and soft. Thus, the craftsman would be able to shape it in his or her own preference without being troubled with the springiness found in most alloyed metals.

Regardless of how small the amount of alloy in silver is, it would still produce an elasticity in the wire once pressure is employed. As such, it would be difficult to work on it for the purpose of fine filigree. In addition, when silver is in this state, it could impede the craftsman's production of silver articles given the stiff elasticity of the metal. Therefore, it is important that all various forms, including the spirals required in filigree artwork remain steadily in their places, specifically when pressure is applied to silver. The spirals and other requirements should stay in place without rebounding. When the filigree requirements become shaky or unstable, first-class work on filigree articles is hardly attainable.

When a craftsman decides to add ornaments to his or her filigree work, such ornaments are enclosed using a rim of plain, stronger wire to provide added strength to each part of the work. When they are placed together, it results in greater durability of the article. Take for example, in England, craftsmen use outside rims that have standard or sterling silver; however, the inner work is made of fine silver.

The art of working with gold and silver has been practiced in India for quite a long time. This is why the workmen there are thoroughly particular in the absolute purity of gold and silver they use. In fact, Indian silversmiths refine silver through melting them five times while subjected to extremely strong heat prior to working with them for various purposes. Primary places in India including Trichinopoly and Southern India districts carry on art manufactures of gold and silver with great intricacy and delicacy or their workmanship. Silversmiths in these places are expected to produce silver articles that are close to perfection. More often than not, the silver articles are handmade and shaped completely with few tools, including blowpipes, a hammer, burnishers, fine pliers, a pair of fine dividers, an anvil, scrapers, and some scales and weights. Perforated steel plates are also used for drawing wire. In India, the process of working with metals, such as silver is simple, but results in magnificent art and industrial objects.

For instance, when Indian silversmiths work with silver, they start by hammering out the metal in the anvil until it reaches a certain level of thinness. The dividers are used to mark the silver with certain widths that are cut into strips. These are then drawn into thoroughly fine wire using perforated steel plates and a pair of pliers. The holes in the steel plates have graduated sizes for better size reduction of the metal strips.

Once the proper thinness is achieved, the wire is subjected for practical skill of the silversmiths, who are expected to come up with the best filigree work not only in India, but in the world. Most native silversmiths also use various books from which they get their designs, although they usually work from their own memory or experience without any reference.

Across the globe, the places where the best filigree work are produced include Paris, Malta, Sweden, Genoa, Florence, and Norway; and in Cuttack, Trichinopoly, and Delhi in India. The finest and probably the cheapest filigree work in the world is found in India.

The artisans in Malta also produce excellent kind of filigree work. While the Japanese and the Chinese artisans produce filigree work, they are considered inferior as compared to the manufactures of Indian artisans. Sweden and Norway also have artisans who produce filigree work; however, most of their articles are lightweight. Moreover, their work is still inferior as compared to the finest articles from Indian artisans.

Chapter 3: Basic Silversmithing Techniques

Silversmithing is a craft that takes a number of years to learn. Today, some people want to become an apprentice to silversmiths while others learn the craft as part of their course in college. Some of the major jewelry and silversmithing centers are found in Birmingham, Sheffield, London, Edinburgh, and Dublin. In order to become proficient in the wondrous craft of silversmithing, practice is an essential factor. However, the basic techniques of silversmithing are achievable given the right tools and with enough patience.

There are various techniques used in silversmithing. Some of the basics include piercing, soldering, annealing, pickling, shaping, and polishing.

Piercing

This silversmithing technique involves the cutting of the metal with a piercing saw. You may use cutting for creating basic shapes or a decorative figures or patterns in the metal. When creating a pattern in a sheet of metal, you need to drill a small hole through which you will be threading the thin silversmithing saw blade.

The blade is connected to handle, which is similar to that of a hacksaw, but much smaller. There are several grades of blade, from coarse to extremely fine blades. Course blades are used for speeding up the cutting process while fine blades are used for detailed articles. Skilled silversmiths know that all blades are easily snapped and delicate, which is why work should be done slowly. The blade is held in a vertical manner while the metal is moved slowly to create corners or curves. In addition, blades are greased using beeswax so that the cutting may become smoother.

A bench peg supports the work, which is screwed and has a V cut so that the area of the cut is supported on either side. Lemel or small shavings of metal are collected underneath the piercing in a paper cloth or leather. These shavings will be melted and used for another project later.

Soldering

Soldering silver and other metals is quite different to soldering for plumbing or electronics purposes. Silver solder melts at a higher temperature as compared to lead solder, which is why it is necessary to have a blow torch. The temperature necessary for melting silver solder is extremely close to the temperature at which the article being worked upon would melt by itself. This is why soldering silver has safety implications given that it may result in difficulty for the silversmith. To manage the temperatures of the process of soldering, it is carried out in darkness. Working in the dark allows the smith to easily see the changes in the metal's color as it heats up, which makes it easier to determine if it has reached the correct working temperature.

Silver solder consists primarily of silver. It may come in different combinations of alloys, which change the melting temperature and usage of silver. The softest solder is referred to as *easy* and has a low melting point. Thus, it is less likely to become damaged to the article being soldered. *Medium* has a higher melting point than easy silver solder while *hard* has the highest melting point of all silver solders.

Articles and pieces that require multiple soldering use hard solder and work down the grades with the following soldering so that every addition does not distort or melt the previous solder.

Lead solders are not used with any jewelry piece or precious metal. This is because the high temperatures would cause the solder to run in the entire silver and would contaminate and make it useless.

Annealing

Annealing is a silversmithing technique that is used to soften precious metals, such as silver to make them more malleable and easier to manipulate. Malleable metal tends to bend without causing damage to its molecular structure, which makes the article weak. The more an article is worked upon, the harder and more brittle it could be. That is why, repeated annealing are applied to make it more malleable.

Annealing makes use of a torch and carried out in darkness. The article is heated until it achieves a soft, pinkish red color. This indicates the point prior to melting. The article is then extinguished quickly in cold water, which allows the molecules to freeze into the alignment they were in when it is molten. This makes the work of the silversmith easier. On the other hand, any work that involves a torch would leave a stain on the silver. This stain should be removed prior to engaging in further enhancement of the article.

Pickling

Pickling is a silversmithing technique that involves the process of placing a fire-stained article in an acid bath to get rid of any trace of oxidation before further working on it. The most common acid used for pickling is sulfuric acid although some silversmiths use pickling salts as they are safer solutions. The pickling solution should be warm to speed up the process of removing the fire stain in the article. Once the article is completely stain-free, you will need to rinse it under running water and then clean it with pumice powder to remove any remaining traces.

Shaping

Shaping is a silversmithing technique, which is done in various ways, depending on the shape the silversmith desires. Tubular shapes, including bangles and rings are shaped on mandrels that are positioned in a vice. The annealed metal is hammered using a wood mallet or hide. Bowls and other curved pieces are vaulted on leather sandbags and metal or wooden doming blocks. Shaped wooden or metal hammers are also used for shaping. It is necessary to carry out several annealing when shaping an article.

Polishing

Polishing is the final silversmithing techniques used on an article once the forming or shaping is completed. It is a process that takes quite some time to finish. The article is rubbed with finer wet and dry papers to discard any tool marks from working. The marks left should be removed with the dry paper.

When there are no more marks left, the article is wheel-polished as in the case of larger pieces such as bowls; polished with fine polishing mop just like a hobby drill; or barrel-polished where an article is immersed in a solutions consisting of soap with steel shot rotated for at least ten minutes. The outcome should be shiny and smooth as well as free from tool marks.

These are basic silversmithing techniques. In learning the craft of silversmithing, it is best to work in a base metal, including copper or brass until the required level of proficiency is accomplished. For beginners, it is best to design an article or piece on a full-size paper. The design should be kept simple for starters.

It is important to take note that piercing comes before shaping, which should be implemented carefully on a pierced article given that it will show stress points that will fracture easily. Once a pierced and shaped design is available, it is ready for a glossy or matte finish.

Chapter 4: Basic Silversmithing Tools

Conventional silversmiths use a variety of different tools for doing their craft. The tools discussed in this chapter are used for making simple articles and jewelry items, such as charms, pendants, and bracelets among others. Here are some of the basic tools in silversmithing for various purposes.

Smiths use different sizes and shapes of hammers to hit the metal to their desired shape, and they will also need anvils, stakes, and bench blocks to serve as a base for hammering the materials. There are various types of hammers and each type is good for one or two purposes. For instance, an embossing hammer is used to elevate positions of the surface when it is driven against the raised work's inner walls. This type of hammer may also be used for planishing although a planishing hammer is available.

A planishing hammer is used for smoothing out any imperfections in the work and finishing the surfaces of silver pieces when they are raised. Raising hammers are useful for the outer surfaces of the work to force the basic shapes of objects. Ball peen hammers are useful for shaping, flattening, or removing dents from the surface of the work. Riveting hammers are useful for tacking and forming rivets. Chasing hammers is usually used for stamping and are available with flat or domed heads. Specially shaped punches are used to press a design or pattern upon the metal. Most of these hammers are made of drop forged steel, although there are some hammers made of nylon and brass. Rawhide mallets are used for removing the marks left on the work. For general uses, a domed chasing hammer is considered to be the most handy of all hammers.

Bench blocks, stakes, and anvils are all include in one general category. They are used for hold the metal as it is hammered. Bench blocks are available in different sizes and shapes. In general, a bench block is a hardened steel, which takes the form of a square and placed on top of the work bench. The surface of a bench block is kept free of debris; therefore, it should always be smooth.

In addition, a block made of lead is useful for stamping and chasing. Stamping employed on a standard steel bench block tends to mar the surface of the metal, which is why it would be better to use lead.

There are other blocks made of hardened steel such as a hexagon block. A hexagon block consists of several holes with different sizes on its face. It also consists of several slots on one side. A hexagon block is useful as a base for riveting as well as drilling small parts of the work. A round wire draw plate may be employed to help in riveting if the silversmith wants a less expensive alternative to a hexagon block.

A slot anvil is a type of block that is useful for the same purposes as that of the hexagon block. Some people simply call it as anvil; however, it is still a type of bench block. Anvils are most used to shape and flatten metals. Most bench blocks, on the other hand, are used solely for flattening. It is advisable to use an anvil, which has provision for securing it to a workbench. Anvils are most useful when secured to a solid piece of wood, as they would become more stable.

There are also hardwood dapping blocks along with their hardwood punches, which are used in making bowl shapes or gentle curves from sheet silver. The hardwood punches are struck with a mallet or hammer, although it is advisable to use a hard rubber hammer to avoid ruining the end of the punch.

A forming block is also available to force various shapes into sheets of metal. It is a cube of hardened steel, which has grooves cut into six sides. These grooves have several cross-sections, including triangle, square, half-round, and rectangular, all in differing sizes.

There are also engraving blocks that are mostly complex in nature. Engraving blocks are designed to secure metal items of different shapes in order to manipulate them easily during the engraving process on the metal. Some engraving blocks are useful in securing objects for setting stones upon the metal. Given that smooth heavy pressure is applied while pusher the graver, it is necessary to have a method of securing the item subjected for engraving. Without the use of a block, it is almost impossible to carry out the process of engraving.

When it comes to large articles, a silversmith should be able to create his or her own engraving block. For instance, to engrave the blade of a huge knife, there should should be a frame to hold the blade firmly in place; however, the frame should be constructed in such a way that the blade is clamped tightly to the frame.

Stakes are made of hardened steel and held in place using a vice. They are available in various sizes and shapes. Stakes are useful for raising the work. A cow's tongue stake is a type of state that looks like its name. A vase, vessel, or bowl is placed over the stake to be hammered into shape. The metal would then be struck from the outside opposing the stake.

An anvil should be thoroughly solid with a low center of gravity. It is advisable to mount the anvil into a piece of board, preferably 2" x 6" in size. Anvils, which have a cone on one of their sides are especially useful and come in various shapes and sizes. The size of the anvil is determined by knowing the size of the work a silversmith wants to make.

When hammering or bending metal, it hardens and tends to become more brittle. Thus, it is necessary to go through annealing to prevent it from breaking or cracking. A torch is used for annealing as well as soldering silver.

For soldering silver, the tools needed include a torch, pickle, soldering block, copper tongs, flux, flux brush, water for quenching and rinsing, and silver solder. A protective eye wear is also advisable while working on the metal.

Basic Tools

Workbench

A workbench is probably the most essential silversmithing tool. Without it, a silversmith probably cannot do much even if he or she has all other materials required.

Bench Peg

A bench peg is used as a staple surface for cutting metal. It is advisable to use a bench peg with an anvil to make work easier.

Tools for Cutting and Shaping

Piercing Saw

Piercing saw is the most useful silversmithing tool for cutting metals.

Saw Blades

Saw blades are available in different thickness or thinness. As a basic rule, at least 3 saw teeth is required to the metal's thickness.

Nylon Hammer or Mallet

A nylon hammer or mallet is used for shaping and hammering the metal without leaving a mark on the surface of the article. Metal hammers usually leave marks so it is not advisable to use them for silversmithing.

Tools for Soldering

Starter Soldering Kit

A starter soldering kit usually contains a reverse-action tweezers, flux, pickling salts, soldering block, and torch.

Butane Gas Canister

A butane gas canister is used for the soldering torch.

Tools for Polishing or Cleaning Up

Needle File

A needle file is used for cleaning up deep or small surfaces in an article. A good starter needle file should be half round, cut 2. Silversmiths usually have a set of needle files used in different surfaces.

Wet and Dry Paper or Mixed Emery

Wet and dry paper or mixed emery is used for removing file scratches.

Glass Bristle Brush

Glass bristle brush is an optional tool for silversmithing although most silversmiths recommend it. It provides an article a nice matte finish.

Silversmithing Tools for Making Rings

Ring Triblet or Mandrel

Ring triblet or a mandrel is necessary for forming perfectly circular rings. Although it is a bit pricey, a ring triblet is recommended for making handy rings.

Ring Clamp

Ring clamp is used for holding the ring shank while its front or setting stone is being filed.

Half-round Pliers

Half-round pliers are used for bending sheet or wire to form a circle for a ring shank.

Bezel Pusher

Bezel pusher is used specifically for setting stones in a ring; although it is not essential in ring-making.

Other Silversmithing Tools

Jobbing or Ball Peen Hammer

Jobbing or ball peen hammer is used for providing a "hammered" texture to a metal. The recommended size is 4 ounces although some silversmiths use 1 ounce jobbing hammers.

Steel Scriber

Steel scriber is used for marking lines into the metal.

Metal Ruler

Metal ruler, just like other rulers, is used for measuring. Silversmiths prefer metal rulers over plastic ones as they are more accurate and durable.

Chapter 5: Silversmithing and the Process of Soldering

Soldering is a process applied to silversmithing where practice and great care are required in order to neatly and properly perform a silversmith's work. It involves merging various pieces of an article at their edges, junctions, and/or surfaces through fusing an alloy, which is prepared specifically for the purpose. The alloy should be more fusible than the silver subject for soldering.

In silver, the solder applied should be suited well to the metal and possess a strong chemical affinity to the silver. Otherwise, the strong and invisible connections may not take effect. In addition, if the solder is not appropriate for the silver, the progress of silversmithing may be impeded. This is why some manufactures are inferior in quality. The best connections between silver and solder are achieved when there is uniformity in terms of hardness, fusibility, and malleability.

Based on the experience of most silversmiths, specifically in doing plain or strong work, the soldering process results is perfect when the point of fusion of two metals reaches each other. This is also the point where soldering becomes more tenacious. The solder tends to form a more appropriate alloy with silver.

In the process of soldering silver, the greater the heat required in the solder's fusion, the more closely the atoms of the silver and the solder are brought into connection. Consequently, this would render greater solidity to the parts united and enables the formation of optimum resistance. In this case, tin should not be applied in the soldering process given its characteristics in terms of fusibility. However, when zinc is applied in the preparation of the alloy of silver, tin can provide a great advantage when easy soldering is employed. Solder made with tin are not tenacious and malleable given that it imparts brittleness that most silversmiths want to avoid. If in case a silversmith deems tin as a requirement for soldering, it is best to file the metal into dust and employ it in such state to the articles as the manufacturing progresses.

According to proficient silversmiths, the best solders are those combined with a little amount of zinc. These solders are laminated, filed, or rolled into dust. However, if too much amount of zinc is applied, the tendency of a solder is to eat itself during wear, resulting in the futility of some parts of an ornamental or domestic article. Thus, solders prepared with zinc also have some disadvantages to silversmiths given that such solders evaporate or eat away during the process and leave almost nothing to suggest their presence. Silversmiths should keep on doing the process until they reach the perfect connection between the silver and solders.

Some silversmiths use solders that are made of silver and copper. These types of solders are excessively infusible for all kinds of silversmithing work.

Solders have various degrees of hardness. Those prepared with proportions of silver and copper are considered as the hardest solders. Next to this combination is composed of silver, zinc, and copper. The most fusible solders compose of silver, tin, and copper or silver, tin, and brass.

In some cases, smiths apply a small amount of arsenic to silver solders to help in greater degree of fusion. However, when arsenic is applied to silver solders, there is a tendency to endanger the health of the silversmith and even those individuals who use it in large amounts.

When employing solder, regardless of its composition, the parts or edges to be united should be free of chemicals. In addition, the parts or edges should be covered with an appropriate flux to protect them from the action of the air or oxidation as well as the tendency to remove any portion left on the metal's parts. Borax should always be the flux applied to facilitate the flow of the solder in the required areas.

Silver solders are expected to be a slightly inferior version of silver in terms of quality. The various degrees of fusibility of solders also have different proportions of the elements that enter their existence. For instance, when tin is the component part of a solder, it will fuse or flow much sooner as compared to a solder composed of silver and copper alone or a solder composed of silver, zinc, and copper, or silver and brass. Thus, tin is the best metal to use to increase the silver solder's fusibility as well as for keeping the solder white in color. However, tin should only be used sparingly given its drawbacks.

In the next section, various solders that achieved success are discussed to allow new silversmiths to learn the most suitable combinations appropriate for their chosen craft or workmanship.

(1) Hardest silver solder with a cost of 3s. 9d. per ounce: fine silver - 0 oz., 16 dwts., 0 grs.; shot copper - 0 oz., 4 dwts., 0 grs.; hardest silver solder with a cost of 3s. 9d. per ounce: fine silver - 1 oz., 0 dwts., 0 grs.; shot copper - 0 oz., 5 dwts., 0 grs.; (2) hard silver solder with a cost of 3s. 6d. per ounce: fine silver - 0 oz., 15 dwts., 0 grs.; brass - 0 oz., 5 dwts., 0 grs.; hard silver solder with a cost of 3s. 6d. per ounce: fine silver - 1 oz., 0 dwts., 0 grs.; brass - 0 oz., 6 dwts., 16 grs.; (3) easy silver solder with a cost of 3s. 2d. per ounce: fine silver - 0 oz., 13 dwts., 8 grs.; brass - 0 oz., 6 dwts., 16 grs.; easy silver solder

with a cost of 3s. 2d. per ounce: fine silver - 1 oz., 0 dwts., 0 grs.; brass - 0 oz., 10 dwts., 0 grs.

These silver solders listed above are merely recommendations. It is still up to the discretion of silversmiths to follow or apply them based on their chosen craftsmanship. For instance, the first solder is considered as extremely infusible to be used by general silversmiths, except for plain strong work. The second silver solder may be more fusible than the first; however, it is not safe for thoroughly fine and delicate wire-work. This is because brass is an uncertain composition, which may contain lead. The third solder is considered as the most fusible if it is free from lead.

When preparing the third solder, it is preferable to apply a mixture of zinc and copper instead of brass. The ratio should be two parts of copper to a part of zinc. Most silversmiths know what their solders are composed of; thus, they would also know the cause of the outcome as well as how they could apply remedy as needed.

Based on tests, the solders that are best for silversmithing are mostly hard solders, although they are not as hard as the solders previously discussed. The hard solders for silversmithing are composed of the following elements:

(1) Best hard silver solder with a cost of 3s. 9d. per ounce: fine silver - 0 oz., 16 dwts., 0 grs.; shot copper - 1 oz., 3 dwts., 12 grs., spelter - 0

oz., o dwts., 12 grs.; best hard silver solder with a cost of 3s. 9d. per ounce: fine silver - 1 oz., o dwts., o grs.; shot copper - o oz., 4 dwts., 9 grs.; spelter - o oz., o dwts., 15 grs.; (2) medium silver solder with a cost of 3s. 6d. per ounce: fine silver - o oz., 15 dwts., o grs.; shot copper - o oz., 4 dwts., o grs.; spelter - o oz., 1 dwts., o grs.; medium silver solder with a cost of 3s. 6d. per ounce: fine silver - 1 oz., o dwts., o grs.; shot copper - o oz., 5 dwts., 8 grs.; spelter - o oz., 1 dwts., o grs.; (3) easy silver solder with a cost of 3s. 3d. per ounce: fine silver - o oz., 14 dwts., o grs.; shot copper - o oz., 4 dwts., 12 grs.; spelter - o oz., 1 dwts., 12 grs.; easy silver solder with a cost of 3s. 6d. per ounce: fine silver - 1 oz., o dwts., o grs.; shot copper - o oz., 6 dwts., 12 grs.; spelter - o oz., 2 dwts., 4 grs.; (4) common silver solder with a cost of 3s. per ounce: fine silver - o oz., 12 dwts., 12 grs.; shot copper - o oz., 6 dwts., o grs.; spelter - 1 oz., 12 dwts., 1 grs.; common silver solder with a cost of 3s. per ounce: fine silver - 1 oz., o dwts., o grs.; shot copper - o oz., 9 dwts., 15 grs.; spelter - o oz., 2 dwts., 9 grs.

The solders above are expected to whiten or bleach appropriately when employed to silver of the proper quality depending on the purpose. Spelter and copper aer used in silver solders because the fewer times a solder is melter, the better it will suit all purposes.

Apart from the solders mentioned, silversmiths make use of other solders for various purposes. Some of these solders are as follows:

(1) Silver solder for enamelling with a cost of 5s. 9d. per ounce: fine silver - 1 oz., 0 dwts., 0 grs.; shot copper - 0 oz., 5 dwts., 0 grs.; silver solder for enamelling with a cost of 3s. 2d. per ounce: fine silver - 1 oz., 0 dwts., 0 grs.; shot copper - 0 oz., 10 dwts., 0 grs.; (2) Silver solder for filigree work with a cost of 3s. 9d. per ounce: fine silver - 0 oz., 16 dwts., 0 grs.; shot copper - 0 oz., 0 dwts., 12 grs.; composition - 0 oz., 3 dwts., 12 grs.; (3) Quick running silver solder with a cost of 3s. per ounce: fine silver - 1 oz., 0 dwts., 0 grs.; composition - 0 oz., 10 dwts., 0 grs.; pure tin - 0 oz., 2 dwts., 0 grs.; (4) Silver solder for chains with a cost of 3s. per ounce: fine silver - 1 oz., 0 dwts., 0 grs.; shot copper - 0 oz., 10 dwts., 0 grs.; pure spelter - 0 oz., 2 dwts., 0 grs.; easy solder for chains with a cost of 3s. per ounce: fine silver - 1 oz., 0 dwts., 0 grs.; composition - 0 oz., 10 dwts., 0 grs.; pure spelter - 0 oz., 2 dwts., 0 grs.; (5) Common silver solder with a cost of 2s. 9d. per ounce: fine silver - 1 oz., 0 dwts., 0 grs.; shot copper - 0 oz., 12 dwts., 0 grs.; pure spelter - 0 oz., 3 dwts., 0 grs.; common easy solder with a cost of 3s. 9d. per ounce: fine silver - 1 oz., 0 dwts., 0 grs.; composition - 0 oz., 12 dwts., 0 grs.; pure spelter - 0 oz., 3 dwts., 0 grs.; (6) Silver solder with arsenic with a cost of 3s. 9d. per ounce: fine silver - 1 oz., 0 dwts., 0 grs.; shot copper - 0 oz., 3 dwts., 0 grs.; yellow arsenic - 0

oz., 2 dwts., 0 grs.; silver solder with arsenic with a cost of 3s. 6d. per ounce: fine silver - 1 oz., 0 dwts., 0 grs.; composition - 0 oz., 6 dwts., 0 grs.; yellow arsenic - 0 oz., 1 dwts., 0 grs.; (7) Easy silver solder with a cost of 3s. 2d. per ounce: fine silver - 1 oz., 0 dwts., 0 grs.; composition - 0 oz., 5 dwts., 0 grs.; tinsel - 0 oz., 5 dwts., 0 grs.; (8) Common silver solder with a cost of 2s. 9d. per ounce: fine silver - 1 oz., 0 dwts., 0 grs.; tinsel - 0 oz., 10 dwts., 0 grs.; arsenic - 0 oz., 5 dwts., 0 grs.; common silver solder: fine silver - 1 oz., 0 dwts., 0 grs.; composition - 0 oz., 15 dwts., 0 grs.; arsenic - 0 oz., 1 dwts., 6 grs.; a very common silver solder: fine silver - 1 oz., 0 dwts., 0 grs.; composition - 1 oz., 0 dwts., 0 grs.; white arsenic - 1 oz., 0 dwts., 0 grs.

The solders above are composed of elements suited for every silversmith's operation. When arsenic and tin are applied as part of the solder's composition, together or separately, the more infusible metals should first be united and melted before putting the arsenic and tin. The tinsel or tin should be well-melted with the mass. You should add the arsenic last and stirred well until it melts together with the mold.

When brass and silver or composition and silver alone form the elements of the solder, you should put the metals together into a melting pot, fused and stirred well and finally poured out.

The melting of solders that are composed of volatile metals are repeated until they become hard, drossy, and brittle; thus, they are not as bankable as the metal, which undergone only a single melting. This is the reason why it is preferable to manufacture solders from metals that have undergone the process of melting for several times.

Chapter 6: Silversmithing and Melting of Silver

One of the first steps in silversmithing is the process of melting and mixing silver properly with its alloys in a melting pot or crucible. This step is also considered as significant in producing homogeneous and intimate alloys. While this process may appear simple and easy to do, there are several precautions to consider as well as some principles required to come up with the best possible result. Should these precautions and principles be ignored, the result or outcome may be undesirable and at the same time, the materials may just be wasted.

Melting of Silver: Principles

The selection and the charging of the crucible, the weighing of the component metals, and the attention required while in the furnace are the primary considerations that need to be dealt with during the process of melting silver.

Weighing

When it comes to weighing, silversmiths should consider strict and accurate implementation. To be safe and come up with the best outcome, various metals that have been weighed separately should be re-weighed in a collective manner to determine if the total weight corresponds with the total individual weight of the metals. If both weights corresponds, silversmiths are assured that the mixture is prepared properly.

Crucibles

Various kinds of crucibles are manufactured for silversmiths who use precious metals. Originally, alchemists associated crucibles with the sign of the cross and calculated them to bear extremely high temperatures. The best crucibles are those consisting of Cornish, English, Hessian, Plumbago, and Black-lead. Plumbago, along with Black-lead is considered as the best crucible; however, silversmiths prefer it to other crucibles because of its capability to withstand the highest temperatures. It is also the hardest and able to stand more frequent melting.

Crucibles that can stand the highest temperatures of the furnace are extremely strong and resistant. Their thickness reduces gradually, which is why it is easy to determine if they are already unfit to use. More often than not fluxes act upon on earthen crucibles, specifically English at high temperature. Carbonate of soda and niter are the elements that usually destroy crucible. On the other hand, fluxes are required in most reductions of metals given that they protect the metals from air as well as dissolve impurities.

Fluxes have various kinds, including carbonate of potash, vegetable charcoal, carbonate of soda, salammoniac, common salt, saltpeter, salenixum, white flux, black flux, sandiver, crude tartar, sub-carbonate of potash, yellow soap, and brown potash. These fluxes perform occasional duties and are advantageous to the silversmiths.

You can prevent crucibles from flying or cracking through annealing prior to charging them with the precious metal. To anneal crucibles is to subject them to extremely slow fire without blaze. This is because the flame tends to make the crucible fly into pieces. When the flame becomes red-hot, the crucible will show if it has cracks, specifically if a cold iron bar is employed. Thus, the crucible should be rejected if it shows cracks. On the other hand, if the crucible is able to withstand the heat, it may be set aside until it is necessary for melting silver and its alloys.

If the silversmith use silver and copper for form the alloys, the metals should be added to the crucible during the start of the operation. It is best to put the copper at the crucible's bottom given that it is more infusible that silver. In fact, copper is the most infusible metal. Furthermore, the copper will receive the highest degree of heat as it comes upwards in the furnaces of silversmiths. Given the higher gravity of the silver, it tends to force the metal in a downward direction. When the two metals fuse through stirring with an iron stirrer and heated to redness, it will result in a homogeneous mass.

If more fusible metals form the primary components of the mixture, silversmiths apply various treatment. For instance, silversmiths avoid adding more fusible metals at the start of the operation; however, these metals are treated depending on their fusibility.

Take for example, zinc, which is considered as one of the more fusible metals than the others. In some instances, silversmiths use zinc in forming alloys to provide a better degree of whiteness, especially if the silver is inferior in quality. Zinc provides such inferior silver with easier whitening or bleaching. It helps n bringing back the natural color of fine silver, which may have been lost when other silver alloys were employed.

However, you should use zinc cautiously when applied in silver alloys. There should only be a specific amount of zinc added to a given amount of material. Moreover, the solder employed with silver-zinc alloys should be more fusible as compared to solders applied with other alloys. This is because too much zinc tends to sweat and eat metals into holes specifically in the process of soldering. Silver-zinc alloys are difficult to operate given these conditions as well as in the production of a smooth and dirt-free finish. When melting silver, copper, and zinc alloy, the silver and copper should be melted first in a crucible, preferably a plumbago, and stirred well together to become blended properly.

Once the silver and copper are well-blended, the silversmith should ensure that the mixture is protected from the air through an appropriate flux such as charcoal, which is the best for the alloy of silver, copper, and zinc. It is advisable to add the flux to the crucible when the metals are just starting to fuse in the furnace. The flux should cover the entire surface of the molten mass to prevent the air from destroying parts of the base metal. The flux, that is, charcoal should be pure and finely divided. Otherwise, if the charcoal comes with a gritty matter, it would result in indifferent working material, which would show in every stage of the melting process.

Once the melting of more infusible metals is carried out, the zinc is taken out with a pair of tongs and placed within the furnace, just above the mouth of the crucible. The zinc should remain in that position until the temperature reaches the melting point. You should drop the temperature carefully into the fused mass at the bottom and stirred quickly to mix intimately with the other metals. Once the zinc is taken out from the furnace, the mixture should then be poured in an appropriate ingot mold.

The ingot mold should be smooth and clean inside. You should grease it slightly and dusted with fine vegetable charcoal. The vegetable charcoal helps in preventing the metal from sticking to the mold's sides.

You should heat the ingot mold to a specific temperature prior to pouring in the melted mixture. If left unheated, a great loss of metal will occur in the ingot mold. The silversmith should be careful not to overheat the ingot mold, as it would also result in undesirable effect.

As with the charcoal flux, it can result in a thoroughly nice and clean metal bars. This kind of flux floats upon the mixture's surface. When there is adeptness in pouring, this flux is kept from coming out of the crucible along with the metal.

In the case of tin, when it is employed in solders or alloys, the treatment is the same as that of zinc. Alloys of silver and tin are not advisable to be kept too long in the furnace once they are fused. This is because they oxidize quickly, especially if they come in contact with air.

Scrap silver or waste in silver as well as of all alloys is dependent on the period of fusion. If the fusion is prolonged after adding fusible metals, there would be greater loss of silver as compared to melting it once. The metals should be placed upon the heat of the furnace for only a short period. Alloys of silver with zinc are expected to lose as compared to the alloys of silver with tin. This is because tin volatilizes quickly when it is heated above the temperature of its fusion. When tin is employed in the alloys of silver and copper during their fused state, vapors rise in the air. This produces white flaky fumes and forms the zinc's protoxide.

You can minimize the amount of scrap silver through careful and manipulative skill, particularly in the fusion process. Silversmiths who are adept in employing the fusion process, make an allowance in preparing the mixture for the crucible. When tin and zinc produce the component parts of a mixture for a solder or an alloy, the tin should already be added to the other metals and stirred well to come up with an intimate mixture prior to adding the zinc.

Before carrying out the process of re-melting, scrap silver should first be sorted carefully. It may be melted into a separate bar if the silversmith prefers to work in that manner. It may also be used as an added component to a new mixture. However, when it is melted separately, a flux such as a soda carbonate may be applied in small proportions to the charcoal flux.

Chapter 7: The Working of Silver

The working of silver is probably the most interesting part of silversmithing. It involves various arrangements and manipulations required in the production of a silversmith's wares.

As discussed in the previous chapters, once the bar of metal is ready, you should remove it from the ingot mold and submerged quickly in cold water, dried, and weighed carefully. At this point of silversmithing, the metal is ready for the process of rolling.

Rolling

Rolling is a distinct part of silversmithing, which is operated in a separate place that certain firms have established. The place is referred to as rolling mills, which consists of the machinery powered by steam and used for reducing metal bars to different sizes.

When a bar of metal goes through the rollers in a rolling mill, it results in a thin ribbon-shaped metal. Depending on the requirement of the silversmith, the thinness of the metal may be achieved by allowing the metal to go through the rollers repeatedly. An individual in the rolling mill is responsible for taking bars of metal to the rollers and watch over them both in the processes of rolling and annealing. This individual makes sure that these two processes are done properly. In addition, this individual makes sure that an ingot of silver or other precious metals is not exchanged for a base metal given that the mill companies do not take responsibility for anything entrusted to their care, specifically for rolling. Thus, the individual or porter's services is necessary to watch the interests of his or her employer.

In order to prevent the bars of metal from accidental exchange, a special mark is placed on the property of each person prior to the process of annealing. The mark is employed through a piece of soap or chalk, which heat cannot remove. The annealing process takes place in huge iron muffles that are heated and kept in the condition of redness through flues. The metal bars that need annealing are placed on a piece of iron sheet, which slips into the muffle. The metal bars remain in the muffle until they are red hot.

It is important that one's property is marked and watched during the rolling process given that there are several bars subjected for rolling and annealing at one time into the muffle. Bars of metals are extremely alike in appearance, which is why they are easy to exchange with another base metal.

The weight of the metal sent to the rolling mill is kept in a register. The register also consists the shape and size requirement of the metal bar. Upon admittance to the rolling mill, a clerk weighs the metal bar and compares it with the one in the register. This system allows the return of the metal's full weight. The messenger or the individual could do other duties apart from watching over the metal bars. The weighing of the metals provides accuracy both in and out of the rolling mill. In addition, this system creates greater satisfaction on the part of the manufacturer and the roller and establishes confidence between each other.

More often than not, rolling mills have slitting rolls, which are provided for manufacturers who prefer to cut stout metal bars into strips for wire-drawing. Consequently, the process is reduced as the older process of cutting using a pair of vice shears is slower and uncertain in resulting into good work. The slitting rolls have circular barrels that are small in diameter. They also have square grooves cut in every barrel that corresponds to each portion with the hollow of another.

Draw-plating

The principal tool of the modern wire-drawer is the draw-plate, which was discovered in the 16th century and introduced by a Saxon from France, Christopher Schultz.

In the past, the the method of wire-drawing made use of the anvil through a hammer. Individuals who used this method were then referred to as wire smiths. The best form of draw-plate has a piece of steel, which is about 9 to 10 inches long, 1.25 to 1.5 inches wide and 0.5 inch thick. Each draw-plate consists of a number of conical holes that come in different sizes. The holes become small until the end of the last hole.

Draw-plating of stout wire pieces is carried out by using a draw-bench. Thinner wire pieces are held in the hands of the silversmith by using draw tongs, which is swung backwards.

An apparatus called a drum is used in extremely fine wire for draw-plating. The drum revolves on a perpendicular pin, to which the exterior receives the wire and keeps it from being entangled. When the end of the wire already passed through the draw-plate, the entire coil is removed from the drum and placed on a skeleton frame.

In the case of fine wire, the metal requires annealing after passing several times through the draw-plate. This is because fine wires have fibers that becomes hardened and condensed, indicating the risk of wire breaking. In annealing fine wire, the process is repeated at least five times as it passes through the draw-plate. For stouter wires, the annealing does not necessarily have to be done frequently given that it results in oxidation upon the surface of the stout wires. If there is a trace of oxidation, it should be removed prior to further draw-plating. Traces of oxidation may be removed by immersing the wire for a time in a dilute sulfuric acid pickle. Beeswax may also be used as a lubricating substance as the wire passes through the draw-plate. Some silversmiths who do not have time to do the sulfuric acid solution make use of oil and beeswax mixture so that the wire can pass through the draw-plate easily.

Draw-plates, specifically for the purpose of wire-drawing, are usually cylindrical; however, they are used different shapes and degrees of fineness. For instance, draw-plates are able to create shapes, such as half-round, fluted, sexagon, oval, triangular, square, star, oblong, and other complex shapes in producing wires.

The process of wire-drawing is associated with silversmithing, specifically in manufacturing chains, in which a huge amount of silver is usually consumed. Wire-drawing is almost mechanical although there are some designs in chains that require substantial knowledge of art for proper execution.

Wrought Work

The true art of silversmithing comes to life through hand-made work or wrought work. During this process, the workmanship of a silversmith presents great skill and taste to showcase the beauty of an article. Wrought work is considered as one of the earliest productions of both silversmiths and goldsmiths. Today, it is still considered as a genuine artistic method although most silversmiths are now using less expensive methods, including chain, stamping, engraving, casting, and enameling among others. These less expensive methods are used for the processes of decorations and ornamentation.

Wrought work involves the hammering and soldering of different articles or ornaments together. The first factor to consider during wrought work is proportion given that the metal piece is hammered to the desired size. Each part of the design should undergo wrought work separately and soldered in its designated place on the article being manufactured.

Modern Working of Silver

With the discoveries and research during the past century in terms of working with precious metal, the advancement of the art of silversmithing have brought a considerable change both in the manner and style of workmanship. Back in the day, the trade of silversmiths as well as goldsmiths was in its lowest condition given that the war on the continent of Europe transpired. In addition, silversmiths during that period were not allowed to produce articles of low standard. Only few people were busy until the peace of Waterloo while gun makers and silversmiths were able to work at their own crafts. With regard to most trades, the men usually did everything they were capable of to earn for their daily needs.

After the introduction of solid and plain-looking work, the process of enameling was discovered. This process added an artistic factor to the work of silversmiths. It also provided harmonies of color. The demand for "galvanic ring" also increased. This ring consisted of a lining of silver and one of zinc. It represents the plain, large, half-round rings that, today, are made of 18-carat gold. The weight of galvanic rings ranges from 7 to 10 dwts. These rings are made of half-round shape. In some cases, a buckle is added to these rings. The outer surface of galvanic rings appear to be purely of silver given that the metal draws upon the zinc. The inner surface appears to be made with zinc along given that only a portion of silver was employed to it. On the other hand, the fashion of galvanic rings only lasted for a while although it had a good run during that period.

Every few years, a change in the style of work takes place gradually. For instance, after the fashion of galvanic rings, hollow work became the next big thing. This type of work is implemented in various ways. Hollow work is extremely showy, but light and appears to be more expensive than its actual value.

With the current styles of the solid, plain, filigree, stamped, cameo, repousse, enameled, inlaid, mosaic, and other styles, it is fair to say that silversmithing has made rapid progress while achieving a higher standard in terms of craftsmanship.

The art of shaping and stamping articles for the purpose of jewelry made from various sheets of metals are produced through the means of dies. The metal is raised through stamping and goes through the bending and extensions between dies in the same manner as when hammer is used for shaping and stamping. The metal is then annealed repeatedly to prevent it from cracking and falling into pieces in subsequent operation. The raising of the metal is brought gradually through putting a number of metal sheets between the dies. This prevents the top die from falling suddenly into action on the metal.

Once the pieces is stamped, they are removed from the bottom and a new one is added at the top. The continuous falling of the stamp forces these plates to take the shape of the die in a gradual manner. The designated form of the pieces or articles takes effect through striking the plates slightly between the dies.

A huge amount of work is now being produced through stamping. Some of the common articles and pieces done through stamping include studs, earrings, brooches, locket-backs, rings, and various types of jewelry items. In addition, the cultivation of stamping in silversmithing has saved the trade.

Today, some works of art are being produced through the use of other methods such as the process of spinning or burnishing. This process involves the spinning of the metal in a lathe to its desired shape through burnishing tools. The process is implemented in the production of large-sized bangles with plain surfaces among other works. The metal used in this process should be malleable as it is difficult to implement if the metal is hard. During the process of spinning or burnishing, the disc or metal is fixed in the lathe with the help of hold-fasts, which could be a mold or a chuck of the designated pattern. The disc turns with the help of the tools mentioned.

Just like in other processes, the metal is spun gradually to its desired form. More often than not, the mold is exactly the same as the shape of the article's interior. Consequently, the mold would be made into several pieces along with the key-piece. When the key-piece is removed, it is much easier to remove the rest and leave the article free. During the process of spinning, it is important to keep the edges free from notches.

Having discussed some of the processes involved in silversmithing, including wire-drawing, draw-plating, raising with the hammer, spinning, and stamping among others, the next section will discuss about the processes that come immediately after putting the article together and the process of soldering. For the most part of this section, the discussion will focus on polishing.

Polishing

Polishing is an essential process, not only with silver, but all works of precious metal. It is carried out for producing the surface of the wares or articles. Polishing should be in proportion to the smoothness and fineness required on the work.

The polishing process consists of powders, such as powdered pumice, rottenstone, rouge, putty of tin, crocus, and emery. The best work entails removing scratches with a smooth and soft dark gray stone. Then, the work is polished in the lathe using a stiff brush. A small amount of fine polishing mixture is then applied to the work. The emery is the coarsest of all polishing powders although it is considered as an ideal mixture for ordinary work along with crocus and pumice. Oil is also added to thicken the mixture.

If a silversmith achieves good work, it does not need much polishing given that the beauty of the work depends on how it is executed. However, if a silversmith comes up with a rough and badly executed work, it requires polishing with courser powers. For smoother work, finer powders should be applied.

The water of Ayr stone is usually applied for polishing. It comes in the form of small square sticks. The water of Ayr stone is used with a small amount of water to the work's surface in a manner similar to filing. The stone is softer as compared to the work upon which it is applied. Thus, it wears away and produces a mud-like component on the article that should be removed repeatedly to discern the progress of the polishing process. To remove the mud-like component, a piece of clean cloth or tissue paper is used.

Once the work is completely polished, it will be covered with grease in the lathe. This grease should also be removed occasionally to indicate if the process is carried out sufficiently.

The polishing of silver is a branch of silversmithing, which are commonly done by women. Although it is hard work, the metal bears a soft nature, which allows itself to be pulled hard against the brush, holding the polishing mixture. The lathe applied is the polishing lathe along with a horizontal spindle, operated with a foot treadle. Some silversmiths make use of steam power for moving lathes.

Once the polishing process is complete, the work is then washed well in a prepared solution in order to discard the mixture retained from polishing. The best washing solution contains soda. Apart from being effective, it is also cheap. The soda should be hot and mixed with a little soap. A stiff brush is used to remove the dirt. The amount of soda used depends on the amount of water. There is no set rule on the amount of soda solution.

Chapter 8: Silversmithing and Enriching Silver Surfaces

The finishing touches of the articles is the last process implemented in silversmithing. Enriching the surfaces of the silver articles or wares is just as important as the other processes involved in silversmithing.

The finishing touches in silversmithing is carried out once all other processes of workmanship are completed. Some of these processes should be carried out in an excellent way to come up with the highest quality of articles. The richest silver surfaces is achieved when the metal is in good quality and the workmanship is excellent.

Whitening

One of the oldest methods for carrying out the finishing touches of silver to produce a snowy effect is as follows: an iron or copper annealing pan is needed to place the work on it and heated all over. The annealing pan should be immersed in a thick borax solution. Once the work is arranged properly in the pan for annealing, it should be sprinkled with fine charcoal dust. Then, the pan is placed in the muffle, which is subjected to clear fire. This means the fire should not have any blaze. Once the work reaches a certain degree of heat, that is, the redness should almost be cherry in color, the pan is removed from heat and allowed to cool.

Once the pan has cooled, it is boiled out in an extremely weak sulfuric acid solution referred to as oil of vitriol. If in case the right color is not achieved, the process should be repeated several times as permitted by the circumstance. More often than not, the process is done 2 to 3 times, which should be enough. The process of annealing requires enormous attention given that if the work is overheated slightly, being in contact with borax, it tends to melt.

Small delicate articles are usually treated with the gas-jet and blow-pipe, which are placed on a stone, pumice, or other suitable substances that can withstand the power of heat. Depending on the silver alloy's inferior quality, it could be hard to produce a good white surface on articles or wares.

In general, fine silver necessitates little whitening. It only needs to have a good color on its surfaces. On the other hand, silver with inferior standards may require half a dozen or even more to achieve a sufficient degree of whiteness.

Silversmiths from East India do not apply any type of abrasive substance to their work. However, as mentioned in other chapters of this book, Indian silversmiths only work from the purest and finest materials, which is why they do not need to use abrasive substances in their work. Consequently, Indian silversmiths make use of natural substances to clean, polish, and enrich their work. For instance, they cut pieces of juicy lemons into slices and rub them in silver articles for a short period. The articles are then covered and placed in an appropriate vessel for several hours to complete the process. In terms of delicate articles, the Indian silversmiths use large limes cut in halves and insert their work in the fruits. The halves are closed tightly while the articles are inside them and set aside for several hours. Once done, the articles are removed and rinsed well in running water. Then, the articles are placed in a vessel of slightly boiling soap suds. They are then brushed well and rinsed once again in clean, hot water. The articles are finally dried on a metal plate over the hot water. The process is considered complete by rubbing the articles gently with wash-leather.

Some Indian silversmiths also make use of green tamarind pods for whitening their silver articles. Lemons, limes, and green tamarind pods are excellent detergents, not only of silver, but of gold articles as well. They are used largely by Eastern artisans for removing fire marks and oxides.

Another process of whitening silver articles is as follows: the article is given a coating of a mixture of 4 parts finely powdered vegetable charcoal and 1 part saltpeter. The ingredients should be mixed well with a little amount of water and applied on the metal's surface through dipping it into the mixture or brushing over the mixture to the metal using a soft brush. Then, the work is placed on the annealing pan and heated on the muffle until the mixture is completely dried and discarded. The work is taken out of the muffle and allowed to cool. After a while, the work is boiled in a solution of potash, which consists of 1 ounce of bi-sulphate of potash to 20 ounces of water. Boiling should be done in a copper pan. This process should result in an excellent dead-white color of the work. After which, it is washed in a hot solution consisting of water, soap, and soda. If the silversmith prefers a burnished, scratched, or bright finish, the process is completed through drying the work in hot, fine boxwood sawdust. However, the sawdust should not be allowed to char as it would leave stains on the work.

In modern and huge silversmithing manufactories, the processes discussed above are considered tedious and expensive. In addition, these manufactories claim that the above processes take too much time to complete. In whitening silver articles, huge manufactories apply a chemical preparation for the purpose of cleansing the surfaces.

Most manufactories adopt the following method in the preparation of the cleansing liquid:

Boiling mixture

Two ounces of cream of tartar is added to a pound of smoking salts. The ingredients are mixed well to incorporate them thoroughly. The smoking salts are not ordinary spirits of salts. They are a preparation of the oil of vitriol. When ordinary spirits of salts are employed, it could result in blackness of the article. On the other hand, the employment of the proper smoking salts results in a fine blanched or matte surface.

The boiling of the work involves a mixture consisting of 1 ounce of the cream of tartar and smoking salts to 30 ounces of water. The silver articles need to be annealed and cooled; and then, it is boiled for a few minutes in the same solution until the desired outcome is achieved. However, if the exact color of the articles is not attained the first time, the process should be repeated at least twice to come up with the desired color.

Another way of whitening silver articles is as follows: provide a mixture of extremely dilute sulfuric acid with a proportion of 1 to 40 ounces of water. The ingredients should be mixed well. The work is then heated to red-heat and boiled to remove oxides from its surface. The fine white color of the silver articles will soon become visible.

For Indian filigree or other fine silver work, doing the process once will whiten the article.

For English standard quality, the process should be done twice. Finally, for low qualities, the process should be done three times.

Articles that have delicate workmanship are annealed through gas. The articles are placed on a pumice stone made of light material. A mouth blowpipe is used to blow the flame of the gas so that the articles are heated gradually. The work should be heated well to make way for the oxidation process and subsequently, the whitening of the articles.

The oxidation occurs through the copper in the alloy of silver. The articles are raised to an extremely high temperature that generates the oxidation of the copper, which comes in contact with air.

In some cases, silver work appears to have a brown color, which is produced as the acid applied during the cleansing is too strong. This is remedied through another annealing and boiling process, this time, in a more diluted mixture. While there are other methods used in whitening silver work to achieve the best quality, annealing is always part of the whitening process. Some other ingredients that may be used include permanganate of potash, alum, salt and tartar, cyanide of potassium, etc. These ingredients are said to be useful in plated work or articles that received pure metal coating through electro-metallurgical process. These ingredients are also used for cleansing purposes.

Common silver articles are not whitened through the process of annealing and boiling in diluted acid. These articles should be deposited with a thin film of pure silver through employing the process of electro-deposition or some chemical preparation wherein silver serves as the primary ingredient. This preparation is only used in plain silver surfaces; thus, they could not be applied to all kinds of silver work.

The preparation is composed of the following ingredients: (1) 1 part of silver chloride; 1 part of cream of tartar; (2) 1 part of silver chloride; imparted common salts; (3) 1 part silver chloride; 1 part pearl-ash; 1 part prepared chalk; and (4) 1 part silver chloride; 2 parts common salt; 1 part alum. The silver chloride is prepared through precipitation from the nitrate with a solution of hydrochloric acid or common salt.

The four mixtures should be mixed with water until they make a thin paste. Then, the mixtures are applied to the work through rubbing using a soft piece of wash-leather or cork. Stirring the work thoroughly with the mixture could also be applied to bring out the desired degree of whiteness. These mixtures are commonly used in silvering clock and watch faces.

Some other solutions are equally efficient in whitening silver articles. One of the most practical solutions is as follows: an ounce of silver nitrate is dissolved in a quart of pure distilled water. If in case no distilled water is available, boiling an ample amount of water may suffice to take out its impurities. Once the silver nitrate is dissolved thoroughly, a little amount of powdered hyposulphate of soda is added to allow the silver to precipitate. Then, another dash of hyposulphate of soda is added to allow the mixture to re-dissolve and precipitate. The solution should be ready for use once the mixture reaches precipitation.

In order to improve the color of silver articles and electroplated wares, the following solution may be applied. The solution needs ingredients including: 4 pennyweights of silver nitrate; 5 ounces of potassium cyanide; and a quart of water. The solution is applied with careful consideration given that too frequent contact with the cyanide solution may result in injuries, especially to the hands of the silversmith.

Electroplating

In this day and age, silversmithing needs to adapt to the modern ways and technology in order to sustain the trade. Electroplating is one of the modern processes applied to the silversmith trade that make it easier to produce silver articles and wares. Although this process is not so new, it is employed nowadays for commercial purposes instead of merely used for chemical and electrical research.

Electroplating involves the art of depositing one metal on another. Originally, it was used for the purpose of industrial arts although, as mentioned earlier, it is now being used for commercial pursuits. Electroplating was first employed in the art of silversmithing in the year 1840 and since then, it was used along with the process of gilding to create various silver articles and wares.

Battery

The most important factor to consider in electroplating is the type of battery to use. It is advisable to use a battery that is inexpensive yet efficient. More often than not, the battery is a small portable apparatus, which has a high but narrow stoneware or glass jar that can hold about two quarts. The jar is also referred to as a cylinder, which consists of a thing plate of platinized silver. The silver is fitted to a frame along with two zinc plates. These plates are positioned on each side of the jar and held to the frame through a binding screw. The screws, which serve as the positive and negative poles of the battery, have strong copper wires secured firmly to them. The parts of the plates that are not affected by the action of the acid solution are coated with sealing wax varnish or melted paraffin wax for protection against destructive factors of the acid in the battery. The wax coating also prevents the unexposed parts of the plates from creeping upwards, which may disrupt the connections.

The jar is filled with the combination of water and sulfuric acid in the proportion of 1 part acid and 20 parts water. The frame that has the plates is lowered into the solution, setting the battery for use. This type of battery is for occasional use.

There is also another construction of battery that is easy to manage and inexpensive to make. It only requires a little amount of free acid to sustain strength of its current. This battery consists of two cells, each with two quarts of mixture. The zinc is amalgamated well and should not touch the cells' bottom. The connections are checked on a regular basis as well as kept free from corrosion to prevent the passage of the current from stopping. When it comes to plating small intricate jewelry articles using this type of battery, one cell is expected to be sufficiently powerful for the purpose.

One of the most popular batteries used for the purpose of electroplating is called the Bunsen. It has a stoneware jar or cylindrical glass fitted with an amalgamated cylinder of zinc. A copper wire is also secured in the jar or glass. In the center, a porous cell is positioned and a bar or rod of carbon is placed into such cell using a copper wire to secure it. In the porous cell, a mixture of equal parts of sulfuric and nitric acids is contained or sulfuric acid only. While it is advisable to apply sulfuric acid alone, in some cases, more powerful acids are required to increase and speed up the action. The outer cell contains a mixture of part sulfuric acid to o parts water. The battery is ready for use once the connections are in proper order. This type of battery is continuous when in action. It has the ability to last for a long period even if it is charged once. Thus, it is much cheaper to use. It is also suitable for the work of silversmiths and those who opt to do their own electroplating.

Amalgamation of the Zinc

An essential part of electroplating is the amalgamation of the zinc. In this process, a little amount of mercury is put into a coarse flannel bag, which is dipped in muriatic acid repeatedly and applied to the zinc's interior and exterior surfaces. Once the mercury reaches a bright appearance, the cylinders of the battery may be used. The cylinders should be rinsed and set aside to dry. Some amounts of mercury may be placed in a shallow dish of a little amount of sulfuric or muriatic acid to amalgamate the zinc plates. A piece of cloth may to used to tie the end of a stick, which is dipped into acid and mercury, rubbing the plates until they are evenly protected with mercury. Then, the plates are also rinsed and drained. As much as possible, the amalgamation process should be carried out in an open air area given that the fumes are highly dangerous when inhaled.

In the process of amalgamating the rods of zinc, the mercury is poured into the melted metal before casting the said metal into rods. The proportion should be 1.5 ounces mercury to 1 pound zinc. The solution can make the rods extremely brittle, which is why they should be handled with care. When the zinc is subjected to an enormously high temperature, the mercury should not be added to it. It is best to apply a piece of paper to the molten metal and check if it takes fire. If it does, the temperature is too high and should be cooled until the piece of paper no longer ignites with the molten metal.

The binding screws and copper conducting wires should be cleaned, specifically when they are already too corroded. Otherwise, they would add resistance to the current, which may diminish or stop altogether. Cleaning these parts may be carried out through annealing and plunging them while they are still hot into diluted sulfuric acid pickle. They may also be dipped into nitric acid for a short time.

When not in use, the zinc should be removed from the battery liquids while the porous cells should be taken out every night. The contents of the porous cells should be poured into a huge container. The porous cells should be stored in clean water to avoid the crystallization of salts of the battery liquid. When the salts crystallizes in the pores, the cells would crack and may no longer be fit for use. The carbons should also be placed in water. When it is time to use the battery, these steps should be reversed prior to using it.

Solution for Electroplating Jewelry Articles

There are various solutions with different combinations for the purpose of electroplating jewelry articles. The first solution is said to be the best in silver depositing. It contains pure silver, which is dissolved in water and nitric acid in the proportion of 5 dwts fine silver, 4 drms. nitric acid, and 2 drms. water. The silver should be placed in a small flask, allowing the mixture of water and acid to cover it thoroughly. This mixture promotes a chemical action upon adding it to the metal. The silver is dissolved gradually. In the event that the acid used is weak, it is necessary to add more of it to finish the dissolution of silver or the removal of the flask to a warmer place. However, extra care should be provided when applying heat. Further chemical action results in the formation of red fumes in the flask. In addition, the chemical action is allowed to continue until the silver is dissolved. The mixture now contains a solution of silver nitrate, which is poured carefully into an appropriate Wedgwood or porcelain capsule. The capsule is heated on a sand-bath until the surface contains a pellicle or scum. The contents of the capsule should then be transferred to a suitable area and allowed to cool. In the last process, the mixture starts to crystallize and the liquid appearing to be crystallized reluctantly should be poured out from those that have already formed. The liquid should be transferred into another capsule for a second heating until it evaporates sufficiently to crystallize. When the entire liquid has gone through the process, the crystals of silver nitrate should be taken to another vessel. A pint of cold water should be added to the vessel and stirred well until everything is dissolved completely.

For the next preparation, a solution of potassium cyanide is mixed with water in the proportion of 1 ounce cyanide to 1 pint of water. A part of this solution is added to the solution, which contains the silver nitrate. On the other hand, adding one solution to another should be done cautiously given that precipitation takes place and if used too much, the precipitated substance becomes dissolved again. As such, it is best to take a little amount of the solution from the vessel and test it using a wine-glass. A few drops of the cyanide solution is added to the vessel to discern the exact state. The precipitation process is said to be complete when the application of the cyanide solution has no effect on the silver nitrate solution.

Scratching

The finishing work of silver calls for little skill and knowledge to implement it properly. After going through the processes of whitening or electroplating, the work needs to be scratched, except if it is required to be left dead white. Scratching the work removes the dull white color from the surfaces, which was produced by the processes discussed previously. Scratching results in a bright and uniform color of the work.

In general, scratching is done through the application of a thoroughly fine brass-wire brush. Scratching is done at the lathe. The wire brush should have a circular form that runs on the spindle. A barrel consists of a solution of weak, tapping it and putting it on the framework of the lathe in order to allow the beer running from it to fall on the brush during the entire process of rotary action. This allows the brush to glide more easily over the work's surface. A huge amount of silversmithing has no other treatment apart from this once the whitening or electroplating has taken place. For instance, silver chains are subjected to burnishing through using a polished steel jack chain and applying hot water with soft soap. This results in a frosted surface, which are seen often in silver lockets and other work of the same type. All are produced through scratch-brush.

Burnishing

Another method of finishing silver work is burnishing. This process involves the production of a polished surface that is similar to a mirror and provides the greatest luster. Burnishing removes any mark from the polishing mixtures and generates a darker surface as compared to other methods of finishing. The tools used for this process are variable and adapted well to the various types of work to which they are employed. Burnishing makes use of two kinds of tools. One is formed of hard stone and the other is formed of polished hardened steel. Burnishing tools vary in terms of their shapes as some are with curved and blunted edges, or straight with rounded points. Other tools are with large rounded surfaces.

Stone burnishers are usually made of bloodstone that is affixed in a wooden handle with a brass ferrule. This ferrule secures the stone in the state it is used. On the other hand, steel burnishers are also secured in wooden handles that allow them to be grasped firmly by the silversmith.

The tool should be moistened repeatedly throughout the burnishing process. This is done with a solution of water and soap. This solution allows the tool to glide easily over the work's surface and prevents the latter from become overheated. The solution also facilitates the action of burnishing.

When the burnishing tool goes through great friction, it loses its bite and slips over the work like it is greased. Thus, the efficiency of the tool should be restored through rubbing it on the leather to which the silversmith has for the purpose. The leather consists primarily of a piece of buff leather, which is infused with a little amount of crocus. Steel burnishers are usually used in extremely small silver articles given that they are finer in nature. In addition, they also vary in form and adapt well to all types of work. When soapsuds are present in the article, they are removed through applying tissue paper. In large pieces of silver work, a piece of old cloth is rubbed. It may also be washed in a warm solution of water and soap. After which, the work is rinsed and allowed to dry in a boxwood sawdust that completes the entire process of burnishing.

Oxidizing

Oxidizing silver work is done in different ways. For the first solution, 2 parts of salammoniac; 2 parts of sulphate of copper; and 1 part of saltpeter are needed. These ingredients should be reduced to a hue powder through dissolving them in a little amount of acetic acid. If the work is subjected for complete oxidization, it is dipped for a short period into the boiling mixture. If only some parts of the work is subjected for oxidization, a camel-hair pencil is applied to both the mixture and the work that are warmed prior to use.

Another solution for oxidizing silver consists of 1 part platinum; 1 part nitric acid; and 2 parts hydrochloric acid. The platinum is dissolved in the acid mixture and allowed to evaporate in order to crystallize. When it has cooled, it would dissolve again in a little amount of sulfuric ether. The mixture is then applied to the work using a camel hair pencil.

The next solution for oxidizing silver consists of 1 part common salt; 1 part spirits of salts; and 2 parts saltpeter. The salts are reduced to powder and placed in a black-lead crucible together with the acid. The mixture is allowed to boil. The article is then dipped into the mixture for a short period. The mixture may also be applied to only parts of the article that needs to be oxidized.

All these mixtures would provide various effects of oxidation to the silver work, especially if it is executed and treated properly. However, if other tints are required, the following substances may be applied based on taste: the articles are dipped in a boiling solution of potassium sulphuret to achieve a slate-colored surface. Nitric acid generates a light surface while strong hydrosulphate of ammonia produces a dark oxidation tint. When hydrosulphate of ammonia is diluted with sufficient amount of water, it produces a light tint. Meanwhile, the fumes of sulfur generates an attractive blue-colored surface.

The process of oxidizing silver articles should be carried out in a closed box. If the silversmith requires to blacken only parts of the article, the parts left as is should be coated with an appropriate varnish. The article may be subjected to scratching or burnishing after carrying out any of these processes.

Conclusion

Thank you again for purchasing this book!

I hope this book was able to help you learn about the fundamentals of silversmithing and its processes.

Silversmithing has been an intensive art that requires a great deal of time, a well-trained and keen eye, and steady hands. Although there are only few remaining skilled silversmiths today, it appears that a number of people is rekindling interest in the craft, which generates various objects of timeless function as well as beauty. Given the enduring nature of silver, brass, copper, and zinc among other metal alloys, pieces made out of silversmithing may be used and cherished by one generation to another.

This book has discussed the various techniques and processes of silversmithing as well as the fundamental information about silver. If you are planning to start your silver artwork, it is necessary to come up with various patterns, which will form the finished product. The different parts of the patterns are then cut from silver flat sheets or brass with iron shears. The metal is annealed and heated to make it more malleable.

The next process is the hammering on anvils into various shapes and sizes. This process involves blowing one hammer at a time to form shapes gradually over iron stakes and anvils. Depending on the design or pattern of your artwork, hammering usually takes a thousand blows and several annealing to achieve the desired shape. Handles, finials, and feet are created using sand casting.

Finally, the finished parts of your artwork are put together through heat and soldering. Then, filing and cleaning comes next. Your artwork is provided with its finishing touches through polishing and whitening.

The art of silversmithing calls for a great deal of concentration and patience given that you would have to work carefully in each step as you progress. Even if you choose a simple design, it might take several hours of work. For instance, to create a tea or coffee pot, it may take a hundred or so hours. This depends on the degree of enriching the surfaces of silver and embellishment. The beauty of pieces made out of silversmithing is the justification of time and effort invested on them, regardless if they are newly formed or made from another generation.

The next step is to follow and practice what you have learned from this book and become proficient in the art of silversmithing.

Finally, if you enjoyed this book, then I'd like to ask you for a favor, would you be kind enough to leave a review for this book on Amazon? It'd be greatly appreciated!

Made in the USA
Middletown, DE
12 April 2021